LAFAYETTE

American Symbols

The Liberty Bell

by Mary Firestone
illustrated by Matthew Skeens

PICTURE WINDOW BOOKS
Minneapolis, Minnesota

Special thanks to our advisers for their expertise:

David Kimball, Historian (retired)
National Park Service

Susan Kesselring, M.A., Literacy Educator
Rosemount–Apple Valley–Eagan (Minnesota) School District

Editor: Nick Healy
Designer: Abbey Fitzgerald
Page Production: Brandie Shoemaker
Art Director: Nathan Gassman
Associate Managing Editor: Christianne Jones

The illustrations in this book were created digitally.

Picture Window Books
5115 Excelsior Boulevard, Suite 232
Minneapolis, MN 55416
877-845-8392
www.picturewindowbooks.com

Printed in the United States of America.

Library of Congress Cataloging-in-Publication Data
Firestone, Mary.
The Liberty Bell / by Mary Firestone ; illustrated by Matthew Skeens.
p. cm. — (American symbols)
Includes bibliographical references and index.
ISBN-13: 978-1-4048-3101-8 (library binding)
ISBN-10: 1-4048-3101-0 (library binding)
ISBN-13: 978-1-4048-3467-5 (paperback)
ISBN-10: 1-4048-3467-2 (paperback)
1. Liberty Bell—Juvenile literature. 2. Philadelphia (Pa.)—Buildings, structures, etc.—Juvenile literature. I. Skeens, Matthew, ill. II. Title.
F158.8.I3F57 2007
974.8'11—dc22 2006027221

Table of Contents

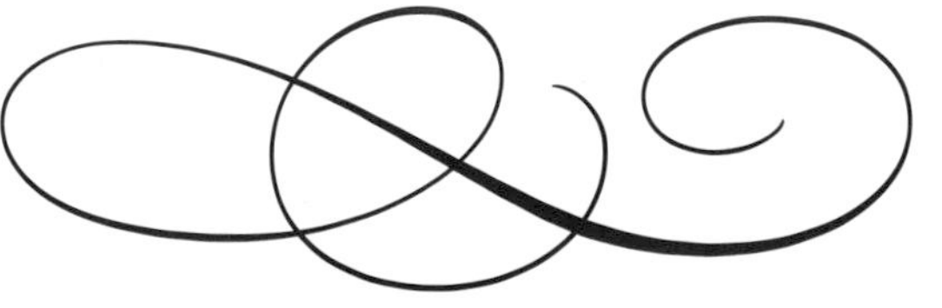

Welcome to the Liberty Bell!
I'm Clara, a tour guide at
the Liberty Bell Center
in Philadelphia, Pennsylvania.

What Is the Liberty Bell?

The Liberty Bell is a famous symbol of freedom. The bell was made when Great Britain still ruled over the American Colonies. In 1776, colonists rang the bell when they decided to break free of British rule. Are you wondering how the Liberty Bell got cracked? Read on to find out!

A Call to Gather

Early American settlers needed a way to announce important events. The best way was by ringing a bell. The toll of the bell would bring people to their town square to find out what was going on.

The State House later became known as Independence Hall. Independence Hall was where early U.S. leaders signed the Constitution in 1787.

In 1751, the people of the Pennsylvania Colony ordered a large bell from Great Britain. They needed the bell for a government building in Philadelphia. The building was called the State House.

The bell was tested after it arrived. The people in Philadelphia found the bell was cracked.

The Bell Makers

John Pass and John Stow were given the job of making a better bell. The men were founders. A founder is a person who makes things out of metal. Pass and Stow melted the bell from Great Britain and added new metals to it.

The Liberty Bell is made mostly of copper and tin. It also includes small amounts of other metals, such as lead, zinc, silver, gold, and nickel.

In March 1753, the colonists tested the new bell, but they still didn't like the sound it made. Pass and Stow melted the bell again and made yet another new bell. Leaders in Philadelphia decided to keep Pass and Stow's second bell. It became the official State House bell.

Ring of Freedom

The bell at the State House rang often. Its sound called citizens together for special events. On July 8, 1776, the bell rang to announce very important news. The bell's toll that day called people to hear the first reading of the Declaration of Independence.

Leaders from the 13 American Colonies passed the Declaration of Independence on July 4, 1776. The leaders met at the State House in Philadelphia.

Keeping It Safe

During the Revolutionary War, battles against the British broke out in Philadelphia. In 1777, the bell was moved to the village of Allentown, Pennsylvania, and hidden under the floor of a church. When the British left Philadelphia in 1778, the bell was returned to the State House. From 1790 to 1800, Philadelphia was the capital of the United States.

Many bells were hidden during the Revolutionary War. This prevented the British from melting them and using the metal to make cannons.

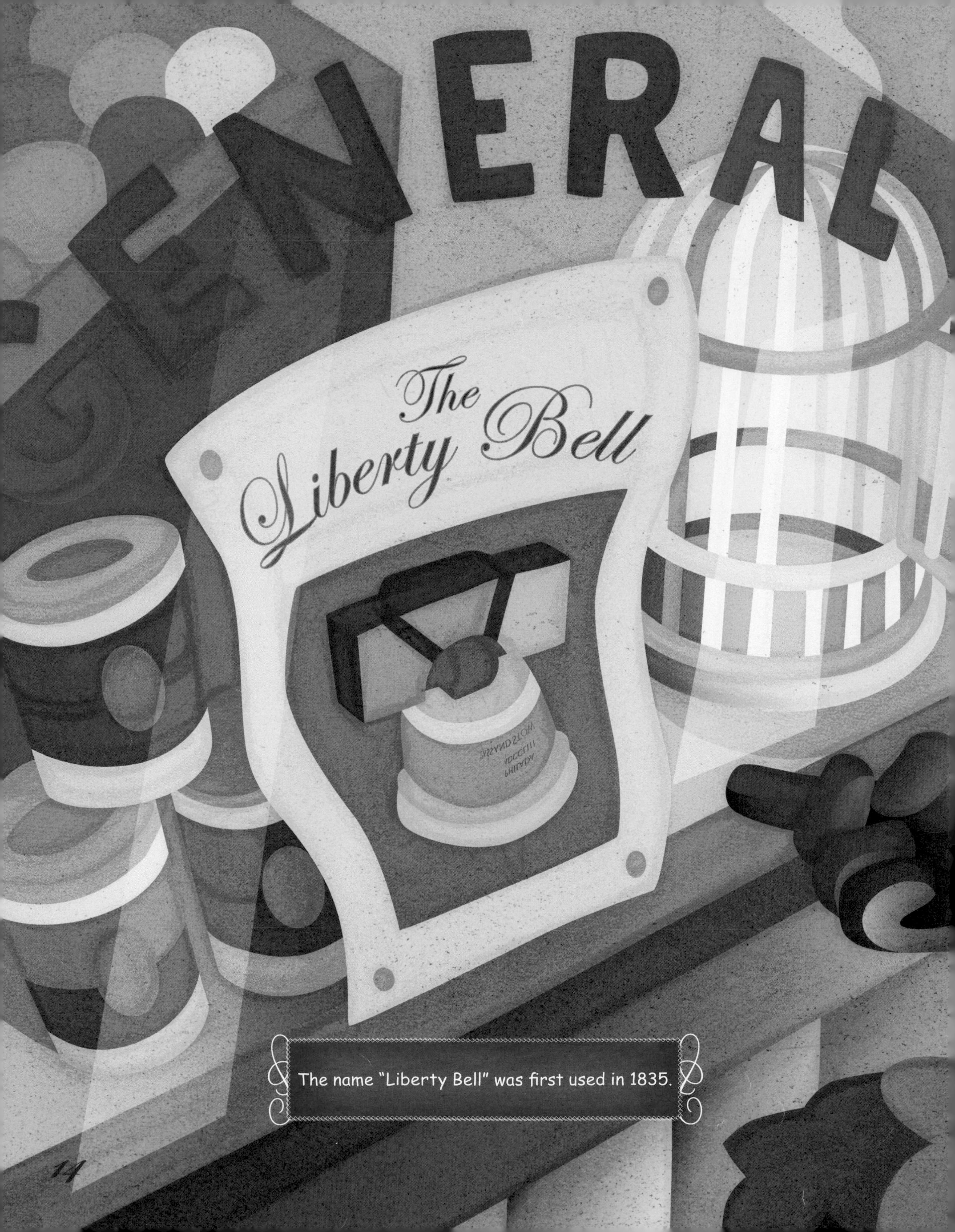

The Liberty Bell

The name "Liberty Bell" was first used in 1835.

Who Named the Bell?

The Liberty Bell has a message of freedom written on it. It says, "Proclaim Liberty throughout all the land unto all the inhabitants thereof." These words mean that all Americans should be free.

In the 1830s, many people in the United States wanted to end slavery. These people believed Americans should be free no matter the color of their skin. They began using the bell as a symbol of their beliefs.

They printed drawings of the bell in their newspapers and pamphlets. One such pamphlet included a poem called "The Liberty Bell." The State House bell was soon known by this new name.

A Final Ring

Each year, the bell rang out to celebrate the birthday of George Washington. The country's first president was born on February 22. On that date, Americans celebrated his birth and his great deeds.

Something went wrong on Washington's birthday in 1846. People in Philadelphia rang the Liberty Bell many times that day. Finally, a strange sound came out. A small crack in the metal had grown longer. The bell would never ring loudly again.

In 1852, the Liberty Bell was removed from the State House steeple. The bell was then put on display inside the building.

LIBERTY THROUGHOUT
OF THE ASSEMBLY OF
PASS AND STOW
PHILADA
MDCCLIII

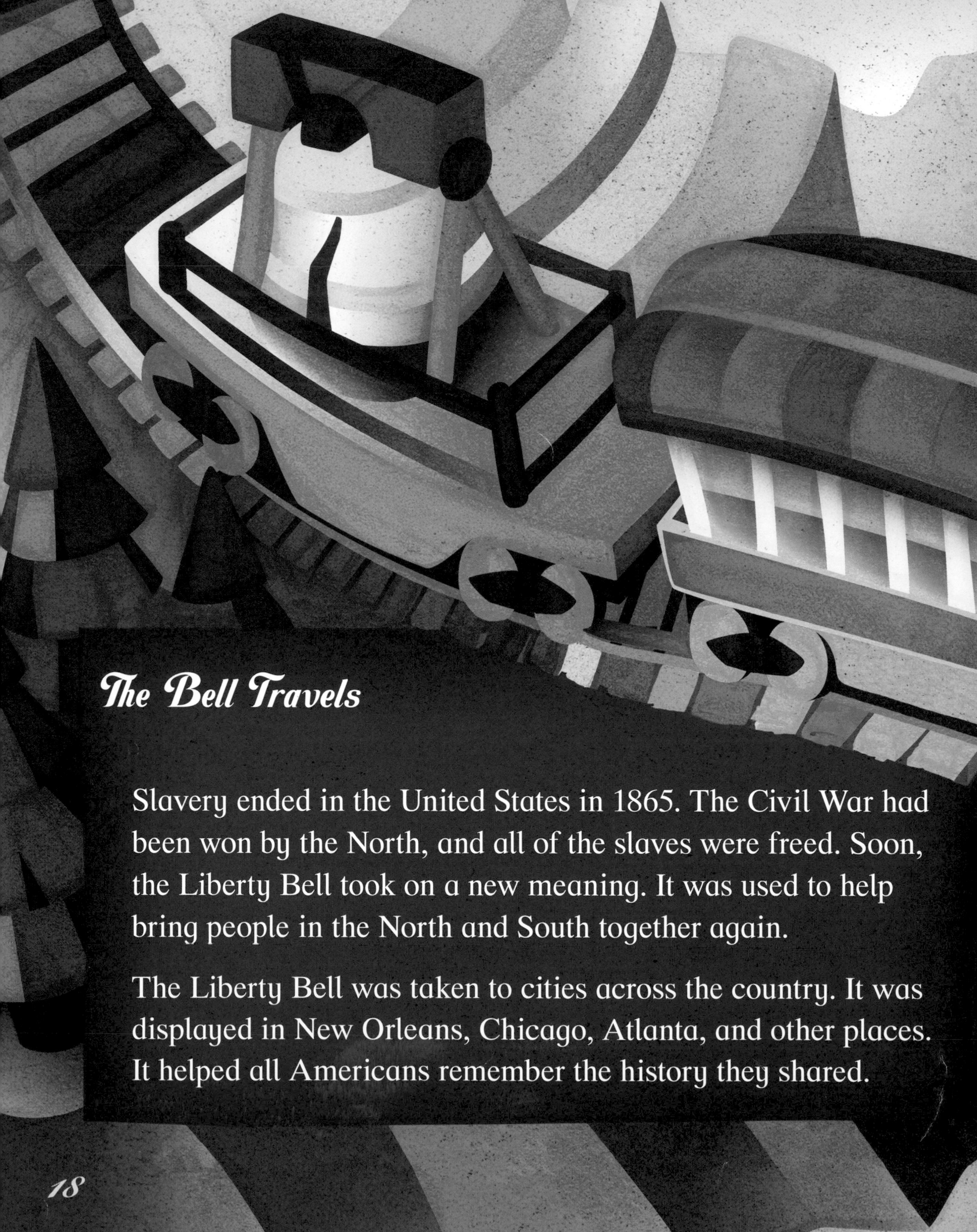

The Bell Travels

Slavery ended in the United States in 1865. The Civil War had been won by the North, and all of the slaves were freed. Soon, the Liberty Bell took on a new meaning. It was used to help bring people in the North and South together again.

The Liberty Bell was taken to cities across the country. It was displayed in New Orleans, Chicago, Atlanta, and other places. It helped all Americans remember the history they shared.

The last time the Liberty Bell left Philadelphia was in 1915. The bell was taken to San Francisco for display at a huge fair.

Celebrating Freedom

In 1976, the United States had its bicentennial. That meant 200 years had passed since the Colonies broke free from Great Britain.

A building called the Liberty Bell Pavilion was built for the celebration.

The bell was taken out of the State House, which had become known as Independence Hall, and was hung in the new pavilion. The new building made it easier for crowds of people to see the bell.

A new pavilion called the Liberty Bell Center was built in 2003. This is where the bell is today.

The Liberty Bell is part of the Independence National Historical Park. You can see the Liberty Bell anytime, day or night. It's enclosed in glass and is always visible. Goodbye and thank you for visiting!

Liberty Bell Facts

- Pennsylvania Colony paid about $300 in today's dollars for the first State House bell.
- The Liberty Bell has a yoke made of a special wood called slippery elm or American elm. The bell weighs 2,080 pounds (936 kilograms).
- The bell's metal is 3 inches (7.6 centimeters) thick at the bottom of the bell.
- The bottom of the bell measures 12 feet (3.7 meters) around.

Glossary

Civil War (1861-1865) — the battle between states in the North and South that led to the end of slavery in the United States

clapper — the metal tongue inside a bell

colonists — people living in a colony or a land that is newly settled

colony — lands away from home that are controlled by the homeland, such as the American Colonies of Great Britain

Constitution — the basic rules of the U.S. government

Declaration of Independence — a document saying that the Colonies in America would be free of British rule

pavilion — a roofed shelter

Revolutionary War (1775-1783) — American fight for freedom from British rule

toll — the sound of a ringing bell

yoke — a thick piece of wood from which a bell hangs

To Learn More

At the Library

Ashley, Susan. *The Liberty Bell* Milwaukee: Weekly Reader Early Learning, 2004.

Murray, Julie. *Liberty Bell.* Edina, Minn.: Abdo, 2003.

Nobleman, Marc Tyler. *The Liberty Bell.* Minneapolis: Compass Point Books, 2004.

On the Web

FactHound offers a safe, fun way to find Web sites related to this book. All of the sites on FactHound have been researched by our staff.

1. Visit *www.facthound.com*
2. Type in this special code: 1404831010
3. Click on the FETCH IT button.

Your trusty FactHound will fetch the best sites for you!

Index

Look for all of the books in the American Symbols series:

The Bald Eagle
The Bill of Rights
The Great Seal of the United States
The Liberty Bell
Our American Flag
Our National Anthem
The Pledge of Allegiance
The Statue of Liberty
The U.S. Constitution
The White House